God's gifts cannot be purchased
with money, it is found in Christ!

ISBN: 979-8-9922853-6-9 - Paperback
ISBN: 979-8-9922853-7-6 - Hardcover

NBeirene Press

Jesus Gives me...

By Nancy Owusu Adu   Illustrated by Christina Rudenko

Boldness

No more room for fear and no holding back!
I am bold as a lion and fearless as can be!
Confident and capable is who I am!

Evil people run away without being chased,
but good people are bold like lions!

Proverbs 28:1

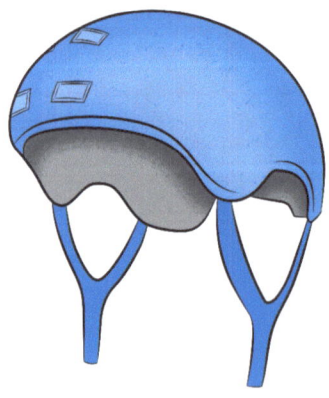

Wisdom

God's kind of wisdom is what I've got
It directs my thoughts,
and shows me exactly what to do!

Your teachings make me wiser
than all my enemies.

Psalm 119:98

Strength

I don't give in! I don't give up!
Jesus gives me power to overcome
and strength for the impossible!

I can do all things through Christ
who strengthens me.

Philippians 4:13 WEB

Joy

Joy no one can give and joy I can't explain!
It bubbles from within and spills over.
It overwhelms me!

I have spoken these things to you,
that my joy may remain in you,
and that your joy may be made full.
John 15:11 WEB

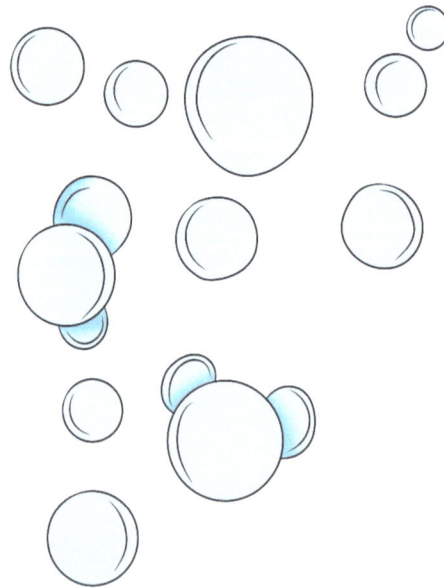

Peace

Even through chaos and storms,
Jesus whispers peace in my ears,
My heart can rest,
for His whispers calms my nerves!

I give you a special kind of peace the world
cannot give to you,
so don't be worried or afraid.
John 14:27

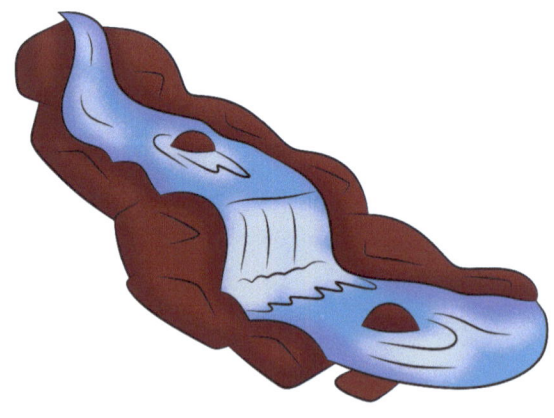

Rest

As I rest, Jesus works!
No more worries, no more stress.
He's got it all figured out!

If you are tired and have heavy burdens,
come to Me and I will give you rest.
Matthew 11:28

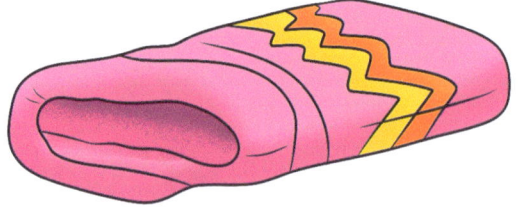

Forgiveness

Even when I don't deserve it,
He forgives me anyway,
no matter how big or small the sin
and never brings it up again!

I forgive your wrong doings
and don't remember them anymore

Isaiah 43:25

Love

Love I didn't earn, Love I cannot buy!
He showers me with endless love!
Love I can't contain!

Your love reaches to the heavens.

Psalm 36:5

Hope

Worry can't keep me down!
Hope rooted in Christ cannot fail!
It keeps my head up and my future bright!

God has plans to give me a good future and hope.

Jeremiah 29:11

Victory

Too late! I already won!
The devil can't knock me down
I walk in victory every day!

But thanks be to God,
who gives us the victory
through our Lord Jesus Christ.

1 Corinthians 15:57 WEB

An Inheritance

An inheritance worth more than money.
It can't be destroyed and won't expire!
An inheritance worth waiting for!

Through Jesus' death,
there is an eternal inheritance promised for
everyone called by God.

Hebrews 9:15

More than I can ask!

Sometimes I don't even know what to ask,
but He gives me what I need and so much more!
more than I could ever imagine!

God can do far more than I can ask or think,
because of His mighty power working in me.

Ephesians 3:20

A Word from the Author

Your opinion matters to me! If you enjoyed reading this book, I would greatly appreciate it if you could take a few minutes to leave a review on Amazon. Your kind feedback is appreciated and inspires me to keep doing more.
Thank you!